MW01036205

Historic London

Historic London

Photographs by Andy Williams

WEIDENFELD AND NICOLSON

LONDON

INTRODUCTION

*L*ondon *is* history. More than any other international metropolis, England's capital city proudly manifests the layers of its past. Its Roman fortifications are visible in the ruined walls around the old city. Many of the timber-framed buildings of the Middle Ages burnt down in the Great Fire, but the narrow lanes that weave through the City still evoke the era. The influence of Henry VIII and the other Tudors is still in evidence in the great brick palaces of Lambeth, St James's and Hampton Court, and vestiges of the Georgian epoch appear around the city in a number of its splendid squares and terraces. The age of progress and growth

under Queen Victoria had the greatest physical impact on the city; much of what gives London its character today was built during her reign. And yet, the charisma of late-twentieth-century architecture signals its race toward the third millennium.

It is this historical stratification that makes London so visually and culturally exciting. After the devastating fire of 1666, which levelled the better part of London's oldest quarters, the city and its citizens went on to produce masterpieces like St Paul's Cathedral, and those who rebuilt the city became heroes. The bombing raids of World War II brought even more damage, signs of which continue to this day. London is a city that bespeaks fortitude, resilience and progress.

Equally, as so many of the monuments that grace the capital's beautiful parks attest, London is a city of tradition, pomp and lavish pageantry. Whether Trooping the Colour, the Changing of the Guard, or a royal wedding, the events that punctuate daily life are a constant reminder of London's past and present glory.

There is no end to the fascinating appeal of London, as visitors and Londoners continually discover. Around every corner, across every square, behind every edifice, there is a tale rich with history, people and spirit.

TOWER OF LONDON

*D*ATING back to the period following William's Conquest of England, this former Norman stronghold was gradually enlarged over the centuries. Always functioning as a defensive building, it has protected everything from the Royal Mint to the Crown Jewels, and was a prison until this century.

BANK OF ENGLAND

*T*HE centrepiece of the City's financial activities, the Bank of England is housed in an appropriately austere building designed by Sir John Soane – though only the walls of the original structure, built between 1788 and 1808, remain. It was his life's great work.

ALBERT MEMORIAL

*D*ESIGNED by Sir George Gilbert Scott, this neo-Gothic spire opposite the Albert Hall in Kensington Gardens memorializes Prince Albert and everything that Queen Victoria stood for – progress, creativity and prosperity.

ROYAL HOSPITAL

*E*NLIVENED by the charismatic Chelsea Pensioners, the hospital has been home to veterans from as far back as Charles II's reign. Sir Christopher Wren designed the symmetrical complex of brick buildings that faces the Thames.

BIG BEN

*T*HE 316-foot tower at one end of the Houses of Parliament soars above the Thames and has kept time for the nation since the 1850s, when it was built to replace a thirteenth-century clock tower. Big Ben, however, refers not to the tower but to the bell that chimes the hours. Courageous Boudicca rides her chariot at its foot.

BUCKINGHAM PALACE

*V*IEWED from across the lake in St James's Park, this monumental palace has been home to Britain's sovereigns since 1837. Though it has been altered and enlarged several times since it was conceived by John Nash, it has always been a symbol of the monarchy.

A ROYAL HORSE GUARD

*T*HE solemnity of this mounted Horse Guard is the very picture of age-old military discipline. The Horse Guards, located on Whitehall, still stand sentinel at the entrance of the building, though today tourists pose the greatest threat.

CUTTY SARK

*W*HEN it was launched in 1869, this historic sailing vessel was the fastest clipper on the seas. The boat was an active participant in the China tea trade, but today it is a museum docked in Greenwich.

QUEEN'S HOUSE

*I*NIGO Jones introduced the classicism of Palladio into England with this house begun in 1616 by James I's wife, Anne, but not completed until 1635 by Charles I for Henrietta Maria. The serene but bold white villa influenced generations of architects and has recently been restored. Today it is somewhat dwarfed by what is now the National Maritime Museum.

HOUSES OF PARLIAMENT

*W*HEN the centuries-old meeting place of
England's politicians – home to the 'Mother
of Parliaments' – burnt down in 1834, Sir
Charles Barry and Augustus Pugin designed
the buildings we see today: a monument to
the Gothic style and the important decisions
made within.

LONDON WALL

$\mathcal{L}$ONDON's Roman past is still evident in the fragments of the walls that once fortified *Londinium* against invaders. Here, at St Al-phage, are some of the remains – Roman bases with medieval extensions – that once encircled the capital.

WESTMINSTER ABBEY

*F*ROM its origin in the sixth century to its celebration of the Gothic, Westminster Abbey has seen centuries of alterations and additions, as well as the coronations and marriages of England's most memorable monarchs. Most of the abbey was built between 1245 and 1260.

St Paul's Cathedral

*T*HE crowning achievement of Sir Christopher Wren and a miraculous survivor of the Blitz of World War II, this imposing edifice replaced a church that burnt down in the Great Fire of 1666. It took thirty-three tireless years to build, and Wren was buried there on his death in 1723.

ST PAUL'S CATHEDRAL

❖

*A*WASH with golden mosaic surfaces and
punctuated by huge stone pillars, the inte-
rior of the great Baroque cathedral conveys the
feeling of vast space, a great tribute to the lofty
spirit with which it was made.

———❖———

TEMPLE BAR

*M*ARKING the entrance to the City from the west since the Middle Ages, Temple Bar is signified today with a pillar constructed in 1880. A frieze depicting Queen Victoria's procession to the Guildhall in 1837 adorns the base.

QUEEN VICTORIA'S PROGRESS TO THE GUILDHALL, LONDON, NOV. 9. 1837

Trafalgar Square

With the National Gallery and the parish church of St Martin-in-the-Fields as a backdrop, this central square – laid out by one of London's most important architects, John Nash – is a popular meeting place for Londoners and tourists alike.

ROYAL NAVAL COLLEGE

*B*EGUN in 1694 by William and Mary, the Royal Hospital in Greenwich, now the Royal Naval College, is the culmination of more than a half-century of work, with contributions by some of England's most renowned architects: Sir Christopher Wren, Nicholas Hawksmoor, Sir John Vanbrugh and Colen Campbell.

NATURAL HISTORY MUSEUM

*C*ONTAINING some forty million specimens, this enormous museum in South Kensington was built in the Romanesque style in 1880 to house the collection overflowing from the British Museum. Inside, the dinosaurs remain the most popular exhibits.

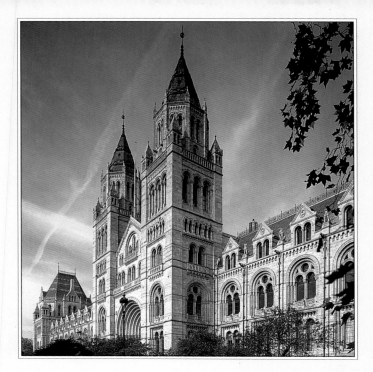

BEDFORD SQUARE

*L*OCATED in the heart of Bloomsbury, this charming square begun in 1775 is still intact, a pure example of Georgian architecture. Brick terraced houses, now stained black with soot, surround the square on all four sides, uninterrupted by modern architecture.

ST JAMES'S PALACE

*T*HE former manor of Henry VIII, the Tudor structure is still inhabited by various members of the royal family. The turretted gatehouse, which dates to the early sixteenth century, gives an idea of how the complex would have looked before much of it burnt down in 1809.

LAMBETH PALACE

ON the south side of the Thames, this site has been the seat of the Archbishop of Canterbury since medieval times. The Tudor gateway, built in 1490, and the 1430s Lollard Tower, clearly reflect the buildings' past.

DICKENS'S HOUSE

*T*HIS Georgian house near Gray's Inn was the home of Charles Dickens for a period in the 1830s, and it was here that he completed *The Pickwick Papers*, *Oliver Twist* and *Nicholas Nickleby*. His works, more than any other writer's, capture the day-to-day existence of Londoners in Queen Victoria's reign.

TOWER BRIDGE

*T*HE most famous drawbridge in the world, this magnificent structure was built from 1886 to 1894. Affording panoramic views over the capital and housing a museum, it has for decades been a point of reference for Londoners.

WELLINGTON MONUMENT

*T*HE triumphal arch created by Decimus
Burton in 1825 – but moved to its present
site on Hyde Park Corner in 1883 – commem-
orates the victories of the Duke of Wellington,
who conquered Napoleon at the Battle of
Waterloo in 1815. An equestrian statue of
Wellington surmounts the arch.

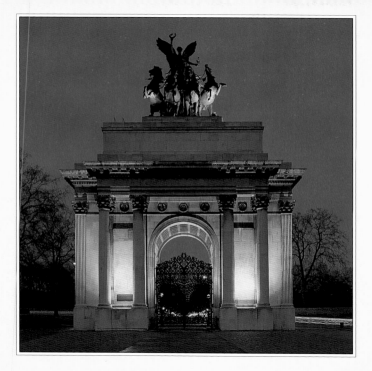

ACKNOWLEDGEMENTS

Copyright © George Weidenfeld and Nicolson 1994
Photographs © Andy Williams

First published in Great Britain in 1994 by George Weidenfeld and Nicolson Ltd
Orion House, 5 Upper St Martin's Lane, London WC2H 9EA

British Library Cataloguing-in-Publication Data
A catalogue record for this book is available from the British Library

Cover and series design by Peter Bridgewater/Bridgewater Book Company
Series Editor: Lucas Dietrich